AF480681

The Modesty and Majesty of Being

Poems to Inspire and Introspect

DHAVAL RATHOD

notionpress.com

INDIA · SINGAPORE · MALAYSIA

ISBN 979-8-88883-641-5
HC: 979-8-89475-679-0

To,

The modesty in all of us,

and the majesty we all seek.

Contents

PART II

The Modesty and Majesty of Nature

PART III

The Modesty and Majesty of the Universe

PART IV

The Modesty and Majesty of Love

Acknowledgments

A warm and loving thanks to my wife, Sapna, for being a patient listener and an honest critic of my writing. Her support and sacrifices have no match.

I am eternally grateful to my parents, Atul and Harsha Rathod, for their guidance and wisdom throughout the course of my life.

A special thanks to my friends, Krupa and Sagar, for always being there, and Janvi for her constructive feedback on the poems in this book.

I extend my sincere appreciation to everyone at Notion Press for their constant support throughout the process of publishing.

I would also like to thank all the poets of the times gone by, from whom all of us have learned so much, and all the contemporary ones who are keeping the poetic scene alive.

My generous appreciation and gratitude to all my followers on social media platforms. Your encouragement and appreciation are simply incomparable.

And a very special thanks to you, my dear reader. Hope you will enjoy the journey through these verses.

PART I

The Modesty and Majesty of Being

The Cosmic Rhyme

How does the universe

express itself all the time?

It is through us

that it sings its cosmic rhyme.

Fire, passion, and grace,

light or its slightest trace

bring out the majesty.

And to speak of the modesty,

it has the silence and the loneliness,

generosity and forgiveness.

It is in us where it is the most poetic,

and within us, it vibes at its best.

A divine tune that is so majestic

played on an instrument so modest.

The Unmistakable Law

When the universe and you

get into a fierce fight,

do not surrender

against its formidable might.

Because there is one law by which

the cosmos must always abide.

It is to reward even those

who lose with honor and pride.

A Stellar Story

What an understatement it is
to think that we are mere mortals
with no celestial relations
and no cosmic history!

Right there, among the stars
and the spaces in between,
breathes a force unmatchable
echoing our stunning true story.

A new evolutionary model is needed
to understand who we really are.
The one that traces our journey
right from the very first star.

Dust thou art,

and unto dust shalt thou return.

And this dust belongs to the stars

that did,

and once more will brightly burn.

Now is the Time

Long have we waited

for this love to appear.

Long have we prayed

to the gods who never hear.

Long have we stood

on this shore without a lighthouse around.

Long have we hoped

for their ships to touch our ground.

Long have we admired

these waves no longer loud.

Long have we stared

at these skies without a cloud.

Long have we traced

the birds in their flawless flights.

Long have we feared

the dark and hopeless nights.

Now is the time

to build the lighthouse on the lips.

Now is the time

to welcome those mighty ships.

Now is the time

to rattle these quiet waves.

Now is the time

to wake the skies from their graves.

Now is the time

to make our own way.

Beyond this horrible night

awaits a promising day.

Now is the time

to love so strong

that the gods must hear

our desperate song.

The Oath of the Last

The day got the light,
and the night got the stars.
The mountains got their might,
and the rivers could go far.

When it was my turn to delight,
there was nothing left in the jar
except the ability to write,
and a lump of lifelong scars.
And under some weird oath,
the last one had to pick both.

The Cosmic Orchestra

The cosmos is singing a song,
and the woods are whistling along.

You are a part of this sprightly band
sent to perform on this mighty land.

Your lips may tremble,
your doubts may be strong.
But their faith in you
can never be wrong.

So, summon all your courage,
and polish your tones.
This cosmic orchestra
is where your music belongs.

The Pilgrimage

The greatest pilgrimage
you will ever undertake
is when you look within,
and let your soul truly awake.

You are the path,
you are the vehicle.
You are the beckoning bell,
you are the temple.

The vibe you seek in others
first must take roots in you.
And then you will find another
to share this joy all anew.

Birth

When the universe was born,

there was a big bang.

All the matter ran with joy,

and all the energies sang.

When you were born,

the moon kissed the trees,

and the stars exclaimed,

"Drumroll, please!"

Fate

They looked for my future
in the lines of my hand,
but storms do not take roads
people lay out on land.

They doubted my plans,
and feared the unknown,
but one reminder I have carved in stone
that my fate was not forged in my stars,
but it is taking shape now
in a furnace of my own.

Shining Alone

Leave it and let them go.
You will shine, and you will grow.
There is this light in you
that you must show.

There are flames in you that you must own.
Even the sun you have so long known,
before it got its admiring entourage,
was just shining alone.

The Craving

In this ocean
far from home,
I am a ship
craving for a storm.

In this sky
promising and wide,
I am a cloud
craving for a ride.

In this forest
deep and dark,
I am firewood
craving for a spark.

***

My Universe

Welcome to my universe a little strange,
full of love, light and a pleasant change.

There is this sun that never sets,
and clouds that rain without regrets.

There are stars that never hide,
and there are hearts that love with pride.

There is this moon that never fades,
and rainbows with a million shades.

Wings

It is the earth that moves
around the sun, to say the least.
Yet our star does not mind
nor does it turn into a beast
when they say it's the sun
that always rises in the east.

There will be opinions,
and people will talk about things.
If they say you can't fly,
that's no reason to doubt your wings.

Universe's Delight

For 13.8 billion years,

the universe has been

in a constant mood of delight,

watching you grow

from dust

to a star

to a person

to dust again,

and so on,

and even more so now

as in another grand form

you are duly reborn.

Waiting for Thunder

What do the eyes tell

when the heart is not well?

What does the face speak

when the mind is too weak?

What does the wind whisper

to the mountains reaching so high?

What does the galaxy say

to the stars about to die?

I want someone to come

who can talk to me such wonders.

I've had rains more than some,

now I crave one raging thunder.

You Are There

All this wait.
All this suffering.
All this darkness.

And then this light
when I have given up hope,
as if for a drowning man
comes a blessed rope.

This light,
a flicker at first,
and then a burst.
Faint at the beginning,
and then overwhelming.
Like the sun splashing on the sea.
I wonder if this light is meant for me.

I know not
what does this all mean,
something of the scale
I have never seen.

The bliss and the fear.
The hope and past failures.
The certainty and the dilemma.
The willingness and the reluctance.
The clarity and the confusion.

But this is a blinding spark
that can sweep away all the dark.
The light and the planets.
The stars and the comets.
The whole universe has started to make sense
when something so special is about to commence.

But still there is this residual doubt
to figure out what this is all about.

To the universe,

I ask why, why, why.

To my stars,

I ask when, when, when.

To the gods,

I ask where, where, where.

And my angels reply -

You are there.

You are there.

You are there.

My spirit guides take my hand,

and show me the new sun.

And then they tell me -

Your search is over.

The journey has begun.

The Grand Prize

They think I have lost.
Let them think so.
But I have not yet given up.
The sun is down,
but it is not gone yet.

When they sleep,
I will be working.
When they celebrate their victory,
and bask in glory,
I will have all the time I need
to reclaim my rightful honor,
and prepare for the new sunrise.
When they indulge in foolish joy,
I will gather my wits and grow wise.
Let them have this little consolation
while I keep an eye on the grand prize.

Blessings in Disguise

What binds me

also reminds me

that I will soar high one day.

What breaks me

also takes me

to a new uncharted way.

What drowns me

also crowns me

the master of this wild bay.

Stormy Oceans

Were the gods just going through the motions

or were they genuinely thinking?

Why did they give you those stormy oceans

in which their own ships were sinking?

To watch you and learn

must have been their notion

when their own wits and courage were shrinking.

Tell My Stars

Tell my stars

to start counting on me.

I am certainly more

than what they simply see.

After a rocky road,

and a stormy sea,

I will arrive

where they want me to be.

Tell them with pride,

and tell them with confidence

to bet their light on me.

Up and Ready

A life full of bad decisions

with immaculate precision.

The head is bloody,

and skin torn with incisions.

And yet,

here we are,

up and ready

for the next head-on collision.

A Pact with the Wind

The wind has agreed to carry
my words in its generous womb.
We will stir awake some trees from sleep,
and whisper songs to some lonely tombs.

A Fresh Bloom

From a bed of prickly thorns

and a tangle of branches torn,

rises a blooming beauty.

Look, a new flower is born!

From a web of spiteful scorns

and the ashes so forlorn,

you will rise like wildfire

and bring a bright new morn.

Poets' Obsession

You may be imperfect,

full of scars and doubts.

But it is high time

for you to find out

that you are the moon

poets obsess about.

Muse

My lovely muse

never lets me down.

She rescues my words

when they seem to drown,

and adorns my verse

with a kingsome crown.

****

The Wind and Your Hair

The wind is in an affair
with your dark flowing hair.
Look at their graceful dance
making a mind-blowing pair.
This is how an old, tired current
becomes a breath of fresh air.

She

She is an ocean in a rage.

What you saw was just a quiet drop.

She is the queen of the stage,

but you used her as a prop.

She is a whole splendid book,

but you just wanted a page.

She is a lioness of the wild.

And you thought she belonged in a cage?

Wildflower

She carries her universe
on the tip of her pen.
She spills stars on paper,
and keeps her space from men.

She grows like a wildflower,
and they dread her divine power.
They try to crush her every day,
but darling, she blooms every hour.

New Sky

These raindrops did not leave
the clouds floating so high
until they were led to believe
you would be their new sky.

A Smile

On your solemn pretty face,
a little smile spreads

like the sun peeks through the clouds,
like a candle lights up the house.

That little smile, that pretty smile
is the loveliest bird in the sky.

Like the rain breaks through dry air,
like the diamonds that are pretty and rare.

That little smile so blissful to see,
like a snowflake it falls on me.

Along the slopes it slides,

atop the wind it rides.

Through the gulfs it rips,

and finally melts on my lips.

Women

Equality between genders,

an argument so roary.

Just think who gives birth to all.

And that's the end of story.

***

The Mystique Arts

The black holes were stunned

when they looked at our art.

Such secrets, such mysteries,

and the expressions so smart.

I wonder what would happen

when they peek into your heart.

Mother

It is a fact to be reckoned
above belief any other;
God is second,
first there is mother.

Her courage is a mighty ship
that the thunders cannot sway,
and the oceans cannot drown.
The winds change their way,
and the storms bow down.

The Duality of Life

Life is full of

optimistic plans and unforeseen obstacles,

epic achievements and stupid spectacles,

bruised knees and freedom to run,

wondrous years and temporary fun,

changing ages and constant longings,

remembered lessons and forgotten belongings,

missed opportunities and grabbed chances,

leaps of faith and no advances,

shattered dreams and fulfilled wishes,

half-eaten chocolates and unserved dishes,

bleeding hopes and a healed heart,

exposed faults and an unrevealed art,

screamed freedom and unspoken slavery,

lost loves and a grand self-discovery,

straight patches and challenging bends,

cheerful beginnings and painful ends.

Poets

Oh! How the poets flirt
with the moon and the stars!
How they shake the dirt
off their bleeding scars!

The wounds and the pain
may keep them awake at night.
But they heal again and again
when the words come out right.

The mountains and the rivers
are their heart's delight,
and this listening universe
just wants them to write.

A Solace for the Soul

Where is that place where I long to go?
Is it down amidst the depths of the oceans
or up there beyond the infinite sky?
Is it hidden behind the bright sunshine
or blown away with the wind passing by?

Where is that place where I can be
just with myself in a timeless glee?
The sky, the light, and the silent sea
would all turn their gaze to me.
An eternal solitude,
for now, and forever more.
My soul stripping nude
on a quiet cosmic shore.

The Kingdom of My Heart

My heart is that kind of town
with messy roads and unmarked streets,
oppressive sky and shaky ground
with lonesome air that smells of defeats.

Dark clouds grace its damaged crown,
and the land is ravaged by flood.
Yet this fortress will never drown
except in its own frigid blood.

Divine Complexion

Do not ask me

the color of my skin.

Fair you lose,

and dark I win.

Though I will gladly tell you

in which color my soul is dyed.

It is the green of the forests,

and the blue of this mighty sky.

The yellow of the deserts

shines on me like jewels of gold,

and the brown of the earth

is a marvel to behold.

A Cosmic Sailor

Why am I drawn to those stars,
to the magic of the cosmos,
and to those galaxies so far?

Why do I always crave for more
as those spheres shine and burn?
Are they my next destined shore
or a home to which I must return?

The Poetic Lens

There is this unique lens
through which we see the world.
A telescope of sorts
to watch starry thoughts unfurl.

A few lines making sense
to comfort the anxious mind.
A shield of solid defense
against all things unkind.

Where the world sees black and white
we see there a hidden hue.
When things do not seem so right,
poetry comes to the rescue.

Flames

The phoenix and the flame.
My heart and your name.
All fires earn their fame
for whatever they claim.

But these fires that consume
should no longer presume.
Instead, they must now learn
that there are things that burn
only to return.

The Inner Blueprint

There are pillars in my mind
that can still fight the unkind.

There are rooms in my heart
that are still full of art.

There are doors in my eyes
that have grown strong and wise.

There are windows in my soul
that still let in skies bright and whole.

Finding the Light

The sun pours its rays of golden worth,
and the moon splashes its milk on earth.
A million stars grace the black sky,
and yet the dark in us knows no dearth.

This darkness will clear
once the light does appear.
The forces have so designed it;
If not in any celestial sphere,
in people we will find it.

A Promise to Return

You made a promise with a smile
that you would be back in a while.

Despite this being so tragic,
I still believe in that magic,
when the sky will light up with flashes,
and you will return from your ashes.

New

There will be new reasons to cry
with every new dream breaking in your eye.

But with the resilience of springs,
your hope must grow new wings.

Every new night you will learn to fly,
and each new morning will be a new sky.

Where the Beasts Have Bled

Deep in the seas
where the ships fear to tread,
I have kept my dreams in a chest.

Up beyond the clouds
where the wind drops dead,
I have put my hopes to test.

Loose in the wild
where the beasts have bled,
I have sent my heart on a quest.

In the eye of the storm
where pride is torn to shreds,
my honor has built its nest.

In the realms of hell

where the devil breaks his bread,

my soul roams to cause unrest.

Ships and Storms

Let me show you here

a ship that never sailed.

A storm it had to fear,

and the storm always prevailed.

Then look at another,

ready to sail the seas.

Storms never deterred her,

and she brought them to their knees.

Iron Will

There are people you do not know,
bravely fighting your kind of low.

They don't cry nor their wounds they show
even after the harshest of blows.

They look for grass under this stubborn snow
with efforts that are arduous and slow.

Their chances no matter how narrow,
they pierce walls with their willful arrow.

These people that I'm talking about
leave not the slightest room for doubt.

You can bake them,

you can shake them,

but one thing is for sure,

you can never break them.

Discover

Rise from these stifling graves.
Dig through these gloomy caves.

Chip away at these rocks that you wear.
Steer clear from this foul doubtful air.

Break free from these challenging chains.
Leave this comfort and embrace the pains.

Shed the layers of opinions concrete.
And then certainly you will meet

a person with a light all new.
Unlike any other, truly you.

Looking For My Storm

For something you desperately seek,
have you ever almost died?

I say, *yes, for one blissful union,*
I have forever and ever tried.

What if you are told
you deserve more but not right now?
Would you be bold
enough to wait and ask me how?

Yes, I say,
Tell me everything true and fair.
Who, when, why, and where?

All the *who*s are concealed
in the realms of the sublime.
All the *when*s are sealed
in the womb of time.

And all the *where*s are kept
secret till you are ready and wise
to open that magnificent chest
that is hiding all your *why*s.

But at least tell me, I plead,
if I am on the right path.

Your own soul you must read,
and your own magic you must cast.

But let me just give you a start.
You've been looking
at all the wrong places,
and even wronger hearts.

The wrong rights, and the wrong lefts,

the wrong treasures in wrong chests.

The wrong roads, and the wrong homes.

The wrong downs, and the wrong ups.

You've been looking for your storm

in tiny bowls and teacups.

A New Start

Every secret you seal
in your anxious heart,
every hardened peel
you do not take apart
will not let you heal
for a fresh new start.

It is Okay to Let Go

It is okay to let go of people,
those who do not really belong.

You found love and lost it.
It is okay you did not get along.

You had a friend who lost touch.
It is okay if it went wrong.

It is okay just to let go,
and accept that this goes on lifelong.

The Seekers' Puzzle

You may not be the answer
to all my impatient prayers
of present and past.

You may be a simple question
that the universe
has so cunningly asked.

You may not be the savior
I have looked for everywhere,
but a lesson
to make me learn and prepare.

You may not be my destiny,
nor my final shore,
but a timely companion
to push me a little more.

You may not be the magic spell,

but just a fleeting glance,

not a graceful performance,

but a stumbling dance.

You may not be my eternity,

but a fervent rush hour,

not a garden full of fragrance,

but a sweet-smelling flower.

You and I may be destined

for other skies and brighter stars.

But this journey has a meaning

no matter what we are.

Or probably, it is true.

You and I

may be seeking each other.

But we might just have to wait

for the next life or another.

A Modest Wave

Awaken me from my lonely grave,

and take me down that road you paved.

You sure have mighty oceans to save,

but for once, bless this unworthy wave.

The Art of Hearts

I once knew this unique art,
but then I had nothing left.
I used to take out my heart,
and put it in an empty chest.

Every time it grew from scratch
with new hope, trust, and shine,
looking for a perfect match
for an art just like mine.

In the world full of artless,
a truth I had to finally learn.
If I kept giving to the heartless,
what could I expect in return?

Fragile Thoughts

My thoughts are a strange fragile thing.

They crumble and scatter on the floor

like the ruins of the fort of a forgotten king,

and the fallen leaves that could hold no more.

I try to gather them back in neat piles,

but the winds of time so fiercely blow

that they are swept away for miles,

and about their return I will never know.

Mother Earth

The land we walk on,

and the air that we breathe.

The light we receive,

and the oceans so deep.

The sky so blue,

and the mountains so strong.

The plains so vast,

and the rivers so long.

The flowers so pretty,

and the rainbows full of hues.

The deserts so gritty,

and the seasons in queues.

The clouds so lovely,

and the rain that gives.

The trees so sturdy,

and the planet that believes.

But the so-called masters

have brought about disasters.

There is one prime duty,

and we forgot to do it,

which is to accept that

the planet does not belong to us,

we belong to it.

Father

He will be stern at times

when he wants you to grow.

He will love quietly,

and will hope you to know.

He will be a shelter.

He will be a wall.

He will even be gentle

when you take the fall.

His countless sacrifices

will lay the building bricks.

When none of your newness suffices,

he will teach you some old tricks.

Your Song

Sometimes, you may feel

that things are going wrong.

But that should not stop you

from singing your song.

If you hold on

for just a little long,

you will attract the good,

and right things will come along.

Of Hearts and Flames

A candle must burn

to melt its own heart,

and a heart must learn

to fix its own parts.

A flame must learn

to survive a stormy weather,

and a heart must burn

to light up another.

The Wall

In this crowd full of false,

I have built up my walls.

No windows and no doors.

For those who are real,

the wall simply falls.

Fleeting Ideas

It is a pity I cannot write

as fast as I think.

One thought springs up,

and another vanishes in a blink.

Ideas in my mind spark to life,

and then die a terrible death.

A new one takes birth,

and the last one runs out of breath.

Trapped

I stand here unseen,

trapped terribly between

a terrain so turbulent

and a sky so fraudulent

that I have reached a stage

where I have to cage

the storm of my emotions,

and bottle up my oceans.

***

A Tombstone

There is this stone
which has always known
what will be its fate.
One day, it will stand all alone
over someone's buried bone
bearing the tragic date.

The Realization of Modesty

I tried to get hold
of our mighty golden sun,
but I was sincerely told
I would get myself burned.

I tried to fly
and kiss the blemished moon,
but halfway through the sky,
I was a deflated balloon.

I tried to catch
some of the finest stardust,
but I could only scratch
the layers of earthly crust.

I tried to set straight

some spirals glowing bright,

but I opened the gate

to a dark endless night.

I asked God with an earnest eye

to give me my universe due.

He finally heaved a sigh,

and sent me to you.

PART II

The Modesty and Majesty of Nature

The Majesty of Nature

There is a poetess I know
who makes the rivers flow,
turns the sky into shades,
and puts up a grand show.

Mountains admire her art,
and her rains win our heart.
You might be familiar
with her fame.
Mother we call her,
Nature is the name.

Autumn

The yellows of the trees

have a stunning story to tell

that even while dying

you can charm them with a spell.

Autumn leaves are ablaze

with flames of their own

before they fall with a grace

no fire has ever shown.

Flowers and Wind

The flowers promised the wind once
for a small thing, and nothing much.
It could take away the fragrance
in return for just one loving touch.

And they have shown the guts
to rise beyond ifs and buts.
They have always fulfilled the promise
despite their bruises and cuts.

Lovers of the Earth

Three lovers it has, the earth claims.

Snow, Rain and Fog are their names.

The first harbors a heart very cold.

The second is passionate and bold,

and the third is weak, we have been told.

The earth loved Snow first

to quench its own desperate thirst.

But despite the bright outer glow,

the earth could not so much grow.

Then Rain began its generous rounds,

and loved the earth without any bounds.

It made the earth once more believe,

until it just simply had to leave.

The earth was in so much pain
that it mistook Fog for Rain.
Fog was a lover so reluctant,
it swirled and curled every instant.

The sun thought to put them to test,
to decide who would suit her the best.
Snow's heart melted,
but alas, its time had passed!
Feeble Fog could not take it,
and it could not for long last.
Rain passed with flying colors
which across the sky it proudly cast.

The Spirit of Nature

Many miracles,
and some of the magic too.
The spirit of nature
resides in you.

The innocence of the breeze.
The magnificence of the seas.
The resilience of the trees,
and the brilliance of the bees.

The kangaroo taking the leap,
and the bird in its crafty dive.
Let it all reach you so deep
that it makes you feel alive.

Horizon

The horizon is an illusion.

The earth and sky never meet.

A beautiful confusion,

and a paradigm of deceit.

***

A Splendid Combination

The smell of the damp earth,

and the scent of your wet body.

The pattering and splashing of rain,

and your rhythmic breathing against mine.

The sight of the dropping silver,

and the dreams of our prospects gold.

The tantalizing touch of the torrential streams,

and the intimate contact of our uniting skins.

The taste of the heaven's nectar

from the cup of your luscious lips.

You and rain,

along with a little playful thunder,

is a splendid combination

to overwhelm my senses with wonder.

A Raindrop

A raindrop

heard it from the cloud,

"Go and make me proud."

Strokes of Light

The sun pours itself
every morning into my heart,
spilling its light all over
with splashes of divine art.

The moon washes the landscape
of my soul so often,
reaching every part of it,
the bright and the broken.

Sunflower

Talk to me
like the sunflower does to the sun.
Like the waves to the moon.
A graceful glance,
a delightful dance.

These earthly things have grown
and found something to love
on a world different from our own,
thousands of miles above.

There is no fear of distance,
no promises of permanence.
Only a timeless story
of love and innocence.

Just one glance towards light,

a moment so perfect.

Just one pull of gravity,

and a gentle nod of respect

will always be enough

till there is time for the next.

Destiny

Every stone has a destiny.

Every flower has a fate to meet.

One becomes a god,

and the other gently falls at his feet.

When a star decides to burn and shine,

it does not think there are billions more.

Every light has its fate defined,

and every wave a destined shore.

Artists of Nature

Every day,

the sun paints a picture,

and the night locks it in a cage.

Every night,

the dark pens a poem,

and the day swiftly turns the page.

Every spring,

nature sculpts beauty so vivid,

and then autumn breaks it in its own rage.

Every monsoon,

clouds prepare so well for the show,

and then rainbow takes over the stage.

Eternity in a Moment

A dew drop forms in the air,

looking all fresh and fair.

So lovingly it settles

on an even lovelier of petals.

Then it falls to the ground

without making a sound.

In this momentary circumstance,

it lives its eternal romance.

Cursed Lovers

The day and the night -

Two lovers cursed by time.

Separated by light.

United in my rhyme.

The Hidden Green

The rain lashes down,
hurtling drops all around
like looking for something
nowhere to be found.

The drops are clueless,
and quite new to this town.
But they rush for their work
as the sky gives a frown.

The wind tries to help
to cover more ground,
and the clouds threaten
with their rumbling sound.

In sheer ignorance

all of their logic does drown.

The green they are looking for,

the earth is still hiding it

in its bosom brown.

Nature's Kisses

Ask the morning dew
how to kiss a flower.
See how the earth is kissed
by the soft-falling shower.

There is an unparalleled intimacy
in nature's orchestrated symphony.

A kiss on land starts
a series of wonders.
A kiss in the sky sparks
a grand show of thunders.

Final Flurry

How would it feel?

Has anyone ever told?

The stars will twinkle,

and then they will fall.

The land will sicken,

and evils will roll.

At last,

the sky too will wrinkle,

and that will be all.

Unbiased

The ocean does not discriminate
while soaking every grain of sand
with its waves.
Nor will the stars hesitate
to shine equally bright
on our lonely pyres
and our gloomy graves.

The sun will bless all the same
the fruit-bearing trees,
and the weeds.
The unbiased rain will soak
all the stubborn rocks,
and the gentle seeds.

The nature has no prejudice
for the dead or the living.
But it certainly has another side
which is not so forgiving.

Freedom of the Leaves

A leaf thought

it could never be free.

The tree, however,

did not agree.

So, it passed to autumn

this gentle plea.

And the leaf gracefully

fell from the tree.

Due Credit

Why all the credit
is given to the flowers?
Without wind,
they would hold no powers.

Like a mother,
the wind carries the scent
in its generous womb.
Like a child once born
gets the father's name,
in the end, the flowers
get all the fame.

Lighthouse

No ship harbors here,

I am that lonely coast.

I have no wind to hear,

and no storm to boast.

There was a time though

when there was a lighthouse.

All the fires it sparkled,

and all the flames it could douse.

It graced this simple land,

and was the sailors' pride.

But it could not withstand

the time and its savage tide.

The ocean tries to churn

a fleet of lovely waves for me.

But my eyes only turn

to the light that will never be.

Fate of the Flowers

One of these destinies

a flower must meet.

Either adorn your head

or grace God's feet.

There is another fate

that will make it weep.

And that is to greet those

who have gone to deep sleep.

Waves

There are waves
that come too soon,
and there are waves
that come too late.

Hardly few
realize their purpose,
and even fewer
fulfill their fate.

Empty shells
wash ashore too often,
but for the pearl,
the shore must wait.

Sacrifice

When the mountain weeps,

the valley absorbs its every tear.

But when the valley cries,

does the mountain even hear?

The river reaches out to the sea

leaving its mountain so dear.

But does the sea appreciate

a sacrifice so severe?

Capricious Sky

The sky is a chameleon.
How swiftly it changes its hues!
Last evening a dark vermillion,
and today a breathtaking blue.

You cannot blame the sky though.
By the cycle of nature it must abide,
which spins fast under the guise of slow
before the sky can itself decide.

Refusal

Oh! These flowers!

They refuse to bloom.

Used to do it for you.

But now for whom?

Home of the Trees

The roots try to hold on
despite the most severe storm.
The trees might be in love with the wind,
but the earth is their only home.

No matter how small or huge a tree,
its strength lies where one cannot see.
The wind may talk of the skies,
and make promises to set it free,
but down to earth is where
a tree is meant to be.

Silent Sea

This sea nowadays does not roar
as if it is upset with the shore.
It used to ride on the wind so proudly,
but no wave rises here anymore.

Long have we waited at this lonely door
for a ship like never before.
The weather is dull. The breeze is quiet,
and this sea has nothing left in its store.

A Dream of Freedom

A bird in a cage

read a word on a page.

Its heart got bitten,

and all its hopes bled.

Dream is what was written.

Freedom is what it read.

The Modesty of Nature

These beautiful flowers,

the humblest things ever built.

They mean no harm,

and they harbor no guilt.

In honor of the wind and the sun,

politely they tilt.

They never cry over

their fragrances richly spilt.

So willfully they bloom,

and so skillfully they wilt.

PART III

The Modesty and Majesty of the Universe

The Majestic Dance

The dance of the planets
around the sun,
a performance to admire.
If our solar system had a stage,
wouldn't they set it on fire?

Shooting Stars

A star had a strange wish.

It wanted to fall for you.

So, another shooting star

came to the rescue.

And instead of one,

there fell two.

Ten Twinkling Little Stars

Ten twinkling little stars
used to proudly shine.
One went supernova,
and then there were nine.

Nine twinkling little stars
mourned their lost mate.
One got carried away,
and then there were eight.

Eight twinkling little stars
guarded the gates of heaven.
One fell from grace,
and then there were seven.

Seven twinkling little stars
got themselves in a fix.
One escaped through a wormhole,
and then there were six.

Six twinkling little stars
got anxious to survive.
One burned itself too fast,
and then there were five.

Five twinkling little stars
brilliant to the core.
One shrunk into a pulsar,
and then there were four.

Four twinkling little stars
tried to break free.
One jumped to another dimension,
and then there were three.

Three twinkling little stars
still in their health blue.
Dark matter flung one away,
and then there were two.

Two twinkling little stars
had nowhere to run.
So they hugged each other,
and then there was one.

One massive twinkling star
thought the battle had been won.
A black hole consumed it,
and then there were none.

The Cosmic Stage

If the universe is a stage,
our sun is my hero,
who burns with a quiet rage
and promises of tomorrow.

No matter how small a name
he has in the league of stars,
he is the most crucial cast
and the most dramatic by far.

All his might and light
he lovingly brings to us.
He is the one
whose warmth sings to us.

It is his splendor and his features

that have made it possible to uplift

us from being the crawling creatures

to the ones reaching for the infinite.

Scars to Stars

The day burns the sky,

and inflicts the scars.

The night heals them,

and turns them into stars.

✻✻✻

The Book of Light

The moon does not let me write
my miseries on the first page.

The stars twinkle and erase
the pain from the middle chapters.

The sun burns away the mention
of my sadness from the last one.

It is then I realize with wonder;
To fight the darkness of my soul,
the universe
has deputed some spheres bright
so that instead of dark
I can pen down the book of light.

****

A Friendly Night Sky

I have many friends
up there in the night sky
under whose watch I grew.
Whenever there is dark,
all of them come into view.

Some of them are very old
while some are young and new.
Most of them still live,
but the dead ones are also a few.

We can never shake hands,
nor can we ever hug,
but our lights always do.

Canvas of the Cosmos

I look up with an inquiring eye
at the canvas of the night sky.

I see splashes of dark,
a universal hallmark.

But I also see a sprinkle of stars,
sprayed deftly from the artist's cosmic jars.

Hearts on Fire

All ordinary planets must learn
how these stars shine bright and inspire.
There has to be a core that must burn,
and a heart that is set on fire.

A Little Respite

I have allowed the stars
to take leave for tonight.
They too have to fix their scars
they got while winning our fight.

Let them too have some rest
and get their harp back in tune,
so they can play their best
and fix our discordant fortune.

A Fiery Trick

They say this about the phoenix

that from its own ashes it does rise.

Who taught them this great trick,

the fire god or a sage so wise?

The answer lies in the night sky.

Just look at a star getting torn.

See how from its own dust and gas,

so proudly once more it is born.

Steal the Show

The stars have signed a secret deal
to make you grow and help you heal.
A galactic theater is all booked
for the fate you must seal.
The cosmic stage is all set now
for the show you must steal.

Moonlight

No song makes sense,

no music touches the heart.

The night is tense,

and the sky falls apart.

The wind tries to sing,

but not a single tree hears.

One little cosmic swing,

and the moonlight disappears.

Tears of the Stars

Even the stars cried

when they wrote our fate.

The night also sighed,

and hasn't slept till date.

The planets pointlessly tried

to influence the pen,

but they were plainly denied,

and have been quiet since then.

Piece by Piece

The moon picks up the pieces of the sun,

little by little, night after night

to fill love in the dark clueless sky.

And then it starts losing them one by one

until the sky begs for its light,

and spends the lonely night with a sigh.

The Modesty of the Sun

Tell me O Mighty Sun!
Where did you learn to burn?

For whom do you shine so bright?
What enmity you have with Night?
Why your divine light everyone borrows,
taking just your warmth and not the sorrows?

I understand why you are this way.
Only flames and not a word to say.
Don't be so quiet about it anymore.
I know what you're hiding in that burning core.

PART IV

The Modesty and Majesty of Love

The Majesty of Love

Why do people fall in love
and then whine about pain and loss?
Why first get carried away
and then send all sense for a toss?

They should know that all the roads
do not lead to charming destinations.
Some are purely designed
to go through intense rectifications.

Why do they keep thinking of winning
the hearts that are out of their reach?
It is the very pursuit of those
that holds the lessons fate wants to teach.

A heart that truly loves

must go through the learning curves.

No conditions, not a single term.

Step up only if your heart is firm.

There will be bliss. There will be gain.

There will be loss. There will be pain.

Love is a journey on the edge of a sword.

Your heart will suffer, but it will be restored.

There is growth, but no guaranteed reward.

If you agree, you are welcome aboard.

The Awakening

When my heart burned,

there was no smoke.

There was no sound

when it broke.

For a while it slept

to heal itself,

and then

to a grand new love it awoke.

***

The Abundance of Love

The world comes to a sudden halt,

the sky splits with a thunderbolt

when you put my kind heart under assault,

and rob all the love from its generous vault.

But there is no grudge that I hold,

nor would I say it is your fault.

Pirates get drawn towards shining gold

like a moth that is out of control.

They think we will become empty

when they try to take away plenty.

But sadly, they are never told

of the wisdom that is ages old.

Our hearts will always be full of love

more than their tiny hearts can ever hold.

Love is a Country

I didn't need a passport to enter
this beautiful country of Love
with such a promising landscape.

And now I realize they don't have
a single ship or a flight to escape.

The borders seal when you get in,
and the geography of the heart
permanently changes its shape.

There is rain of affection here,
and also rivers of tears.
Caves of despair, and a farmhouse near.

There is monarchy in this kingdom,

and the one you love rules.

Lots of lessons, but no schools.

Whether you think it's bad or good,

Love is a country frequently visited,

but seldom understood.

Secrets and Love

The world is full of secrets,
some forgotten, some untold.
Some we will miss in plain sight,
and some we must slowly unfold.

The world is full of love.
It may grace you with warmth
or it may turn you stone-cold.
Some of it will slip right through your fingers,
and some of it you will forever hold.

Pen and Paper

What a remarkable love story
Pen and Paper have, full of glory!
They cannot stay together lifelong
despite the bond being really strong.
Yet the Pen gives everything
with all its lovely craftiness,
and selflessly saves the Paper
from its lifelong emptiness.

Seasons of Love

The life cycle of love
is like the roll of the seasons.

There is warmth when you require,
and the heat of fiery desire.
The coldness of romantic inaction,
and the freezing of promised affection.

A soft-falling shower with rainbow
or a crazy storm with heavy snow.
There is autumn of misunderstandings
followed by the spring of new beginnings.

If the love is pure and meant well,
the whole process is just awesome.
Because after every dry spell,
there always is a new blossom.

The Shape of Your Soul

Why do you keep changing

the shape of your soul

to fit the wrong ones?

The right one will embrace you

with the swiftness of a fluid

and the gravity of a thousand suns.

Transformation

Love is not a fixed deposit
where you always get a return.
It is a fire passionately lit
in which hearts selflessly burn.

Love is not a transaction
that involves simple give and take.
It is a sea of transformation
in which sleepy sailors awake.

Savior

After constant defeats
what still remains,
you are that fight.

After several wrongs
what finally rescues,
you are that right.

After a painful day
what gives peace,
you are that night.

After endless wandering
what brings an asteroid into an orbit,
you are that might.

After the darkest of times

what the moon brings,

you are that light.

A Shine of Your Own

I made you my sky,

but you started changing colors.

I made you my moon,

but you swung between phases.

I made you my sun,

but you had to be away at night.

So, I let you be yourself,

and you lit up with a constant light.

Rainbow

Whenever this pen touched paper,

it left on them just blots and stains.

You turned it into a rich cloud

from where now divine poetry rains.

My rainbow was incomplete.

It was as good as dead.

My blue was meaningless

until you gave me your red.

The Coming of the Storm

When the lightning strikes,

I will call out your name.

I will think of you

when the clouds play their game.

Because the storm reminds me

of the way you came.

An Earnest Request

O Wind! Be gentle to her
like when you speak to a tree.
She has already faced mine,
so now, bring her storms to me.

O Thunder! Be quiet for a while
like when you let the clouds weep.
She has stayed awake for miles,
so now, let her peacefully sleep.

O Earth! Be generous to her
like when you nourish the seeds.
She would always give selflessly,
so now, you look after her needs.

The Meeting

You were fishing for a star
in the sea of this night sky.
Some seemed really far
while some missed your farsighted eye.

By a pure chance of some sort,
you caught a falling comet.
And that is the long story short
how you and I finally met.

Treasure

You opened up your heart bare,

and mine started to race.

I looked for some love there

or just even a slight trace.

I found a treasure where

others just saw empty space.

***

The Light of Love

Your love ends the dark

at the break of day.

It is the benchmark

that shows me the way.

The thoughts of you

every afternoon,

on the days so blue,

are a much-needed boon.

The glimpse of your face

under the setting sun

is my well-earned grace

when the day is done.

The warmth in your arms
at the fall of night
is the best of charms
and my most sought delight.

A Mighty Fire

I will leave no stone unturned
to love you like no one has,
like no fire has ever burned,
and no star has been ablaze.

Oh! Please, do not let this love die.
Something nurtured by you and I
must outlive the age of the stars,
and even make the mountains shy.

The Joy of Loving You

You ask what your love is to me,
and I think all things it can be.
As high as the lofty mountains,
and as deep as the bottomless sea.

The eighth color of the rainbow,
and the ninth cloud in the sky,
the light of the sparkling snow,
and the joy of birds flying by.

The Auburn of Autumn

The wind tries to catch

the ends of your playful hair.

It knows there is no match

for something so precious and rare.

To live up to your auburn strands,

the autumn sets the trees ablaze.

Fiery shades cover the dry lands,

and the air fills up with jealous daze.

In an Imperfect World

In a world that was perfect,
you and I would not have met.

With all the flaws that we possess,
and the minds that are total mess,
the untold secrets yet to confess,
and the feelings so hard to express.

In a perfect world,
these would not exist,
forcing us apart
in a blinding mist.

It was in the chaos
of this worldly fate
that we chanced upon love
amidst all this hate.

A Mighty Force

Why is it a practice
so common and well-known
that you seek other hearts
to discover your own?

Why is it not understood
that a soul that has grown alone
is a mighty display of force
that two could never have shown?

You and I

You and I,

a constellation out of shape,

two stars that could not unite

nor could escape.

You and I,

a troubled, unruly landscape

with the mountains so possessive

that the rivers could not escape.

Heart's Doors

We are different

behind our heart's doors.

Soft spots in mine.

Hard feelings in yours.

They know different knocks.

They answer to different calls.

Yours is studded with locks,

and mine is even coming off its walls.

The Perfect Place

If you are looking for the sun,

I may not be the one.

If you are looking for the moon,

I may have to leave too soon.

If you are looking for a star,

you will have to look a little far.

If you are looking for a cloud,

I may not make you proud.

If you are looking for the sky,

I may not rise so high.

But if, in me,

you are looking for your own trace,

then, my love,

you have come to the perfect place.

The Embroidery of Hearts

No one has yet fully known
the art of this kind of repair.
Every heart is on its own
to pull itself out of despair.

Give me a needle and enough of thread,
and another magical yarn of love I will weave.
Stitch my wounds, and sew fast the shreds
and then perhaps, again I will believe.

Truth and Lies

What if one day
the sun just forgets to rise
and the earth misses its spin?

The moon stops changing its size
and the color of its skin.

Lost clouds wander the gloomy skies
with no raindrop left within.

The mountains give up their highs,
and the rivers grow so thin.

On that day,
will you stop all your lies
so that our truth can begin?

No Other Fate

Whether I become soft rain

or cold-hearted snow.

I would always fall for you.

There is no other fate I know.

✹✹✹

A Wish to Be Loved

I wish I could fit myself

in your generous bookshelf.

I would adjust in a small space

just to feel your fingers trace

down my long starving spine

with the love that could never be mine.

My Heart as a Home

You can make my heart your home

or you may just enter as a thief.

But before you decide to come,

I must tell you in brief

that the roof is leaking,

the floor has got a cracked voice,

and the walls have stopped speaking.

The doors and windows are shut tight,

and the rooms have lost their appeal.

You might not like it, or you might,

but as a home, it would be a bad deal.

And if you choose to burgle it one night,

you'll find there is nothing left to steal.

Acquisition and Estrangement

I listened to you

like one learns new music.

Now, even my name from your tongue

seems to be out of tune.

I loved you

like one absorbs a new language.

Now, even your name

sounds foreign in my mouth.

A Messy Tangle

A messy tangle we were,

you and I,

of fully-naked truths

and half-baked lies.

Our love,

a tale of no blessings, only disguise,

pains of every proportion,

and sins of every size.

Stubborn Fog

Winter's cold breath chills my spine.

No love warms me, nor any wine.

Two kinds of fog there are:

One mists this world,

and the other clouds your heart.

The first one is gentler,

and it lifts when the sun comes out,

but the other one is stubborn,

filled with shadows of doubt.

No light can sneak through that domain,

and there no star asserts its reign.

Not For Me

She is not so tall.

She is not so slim.

Her heart is full of light,

and mind full of whim.

I love her like crazy,

but she is made for him.

She is a moon person,

otherwise my sun is not so dim.

My stars are in my favor,

but hers are aligned just for him.

Stolen

Something has been taken
from the cage of my chest.
Left is a pump forsaken,
you pulled out the rest.

There is no peace to find,
and gone is all the relief.
It is true that love is blind,
because I loved a thief.

Cover-up

The sky does not speak
of my stars' wounded pride,
and the moon covers the matter
with every rising tide.

The days never reveal,
and the nights always hide
the love that lived,
and the promise that died.

Fragile Love

Your pride high in the sky,

and my heart down on its knees.

The stars went so quiet,

and roaring were the seas.

The nights got treacherous,

and the days ignored my pleas.

Our love could not stand

even the gentlest of a breeze.

Where I had watered the land,

you just uprooted those trees.

Cracks

The cracks in my heart

are an odd landscape.

They are too small

to let you escape,

and yet too large

to get back in shape.

***

Love is a Ghost

It is a thought quite daunting

that love is a silly old ghost

whose art of haunting

seems to have been lost.

It visits as a guest,

and just briefly troubles the host.

And it scares its best

where it is valued the most.

A Ruined Dance

Falling for you at first glance

was an act full of grace.

The culprit for our ruined dance

was your heart out of place.

Your fake love will keep me alive,

and my pure heart you will cherish.

With my truth, I will survive,

but in your lies, you will perish.

The Lows of Heartbreak

The stars do not deliver
their light where I am so lost.
Here the moon cries a river,
and the sun grieves the most.

Darkness reigns supreme,
and sanity has no share.
What once was a living dream
is now a deadly nightmare.

Inadequate

The moonlight you stole
from my sparkling soul,
the sunlight you charmed
out of my festive heart,
were they not adequate
to seal our fragile fate?

Unloving

There were ten things
I liked about you.
All those common things,
and nothing so new.

First, your beautiful eyes
lost that beautiful shine.
Perhaps I stopped seeing it,
and then there were nine.

You then confessed
you didn't believe in fate.
Maybe it was our destiny,
and then there were eight.

I loved you for what you were,
with your whole past forgiven.
But you didn't return the favor,
and then there were seven.

Your heart was so innocent
before it played all its tricks.
I became the victim,
and then there were six.

Your gentle loving touch
turned all my senses alive.
But then you scratched my heart,
and then there were five.

Love cannot be measured,
but you started keeping a score.
I kept a different count,
and then there were four.

I never possessed you,

but you never set me free.

I lost my real self,

and then there were three.

We disregarded the rumors,

and sought what was true.

But you believed one about me,

and then there were two.

Your light showed me a path,

and you warmed me like the sun.

But you soon ran out of fuel,

and then there was one.

All the efforts ceased,

and all the threads came undone.

Ten things there used to be,

and then there were none.

Your Smile

A sudden gush of pleasant breeze.

An outpouring of streams.

An explosive burst of sunshine.

A manifestation of dreams.

Your long enigmatic smile,

and those deep revealing eyes.

Was that an answer to all my questions

or another mystery in disguise?

Our Little Secret

In the sky full of stars,

I look for your shine.

On this night fully dark,

I know you are not mine.

In this life full of misery,

and this heart filled with regrets

will live forever our little secret.

An Unanswerable Question

At first,

love effortlessly flows,

then it grows,

and brightly glows.

When it passes through the lows,

just away it blows.

'Why?' you ask.

Well, that ... nobody knows.

A Modest Beginning

The tumbling of the book

from your hand,

and onto the floor

miraculously opened

a great new door.

I picked it up,

and studied the title

to see if it was relevant

to this encounter so vital.

I gave it back to you,

and our eyes met,

with our hearts racing

and the palms wet.

It was a book
I had never read,
but it started a story
nobody had ever said.

Set the Words Free

Trapped are your words
like some caged birds.

Set them free,
and let them find their own way
straight to me
to tell me all you could never say.

I beg you to see
that these words you have imprisoned
hold the only key
to the love we have envisioned.

Intimacy

Let me be all those lovely things
which snugly to your body cling.

Your sweater, your diary, your book,
the red heart in your bracelet hook.

That floral tiara on your head,
and the pillow of your cozy bed.

Through the breezy nights,
and the stormy days,
let me hug you
in a million different ways.

Unconditional

The rarity,

the scarcity,

the modesty,

and the majesty

of the unconditional.

What happened to that kind of love?

Why do we no longer believe?

Why do we hesitate to give

where there is no scope to receive?

The Real Jewel

Every breath, every moment of our love
I pulled together to make a necklace.
But it took just one sudden motion for you
to snap the string in a manner so reckless.

Now I am picking up the pearls one by one
to stitch it whole again what you have undone.

The beads do not align,
broken is the thread.
They give me a sign
not to go ahead.
So, I turn to refine
my own heart instead.

The Seed of Light

They say the universe is expanding.

Even the stars

that wrote my fate

are drifting away.

How could I expect you to stay?

The light that I see

flickering in the night sky

is not just fleeing from me,

but is also long dead.

The red shift of the stars

echo the moments

when I last saw you in red.

And yet,

this last of the light is so powerful

that rather than bury,

I choose to plant it instead.

The Modesty of the Soul

If I am a tree,

you are the soil

that makes me grow.

If I am the moon,

you are the sun

with whose light I glow.

If I am fragrance,

you are a flower so rare.

Without you,

I am just plain empty air.

You are the earth,

and I am rain.

For you I fall,

again and again.

If I am a mountain,

will you be my vale?

Without your depth,

my heights are so pale.

If you are lips,

I am the joyous laugh.

You are a seeker,

and I am your other half.

A New Love Awaits

The clouds of dark love
have slowly drifted.
The grounds of shaky trust
have gradually shifted.
A new blessed love
will claim its rightful place,
and that ugly old curse
will be finally lifted.

The Modesty in Loving Yourself

The only reason

I look up at the stars

is to remind myself

just how far you are.

The only reason

I look down in the lake

is to teach myself

that even the sky can be fake.

The only reason

I look within my soul

is to learn the fact

that alone can also be whole.